for my friend
Geri Evans
one of the many good
thing from TH — y
friendship —
Ken Lee
4-22-99

John Adam Treutlen

Georgia's First Constitutional Governor
His Life, Real and Rumored

Edna Q. Morgan

Historic Effingham Society, Inc.
Springfield, Georgia
1998

Edna Q. Morgan
    John Adam Treutlen, Georgia's first constitutional governor, his life, real and rumored

ISBN 0-9669559-0-0

1. History, Georgia, 18th century. 2. History, South Carolina, 18th Century. 3. Social conditions. 4. Political conditions.

Library of Congress Catalog Card Number 98-75823

Copies of this publication may be ordered from the Historic Effingham Society, Inc., P.O. Box 999, Springfield, GA 31329. Enclose $22.50 to include cost of book plus shipping. If you are a resident of Georgia, please add $1.40 sales tax.

To the memory of
REBAH MALLORY
who diligently collected most of
the material used in this book

CONTENTS

Foreword

FOREWORD

This project began merely as an attempt to combine into one article the seventeen articles and ten letters Miss Rebah Mallory had collected, together with the numerous articles she had written about her illustrious ancestor, John Adam Treutlen. After Miss Mallory's death these writings were given to the Historic Effingham Society for preservation in the Old Jail Museum. Volunteers at the museum had placed all the information except the magazines in protective sleeves in a three-ring notebook binder. Knowing that few people would take the time to read all these articles, they asked this writer to condense the material for easier reading.

Later, when members of the Executive Committee Board of Historic Effingham Society realized that few, if any, works devoted mainly to the life of John Adam Treutlen exist, they decided that such a book should be published. With this in mind, this writer began to research other sources of information about Treutlen and to incorporate it into the original text.

When one board member of the society submitted a copy of the work to Dr. George Fenwick Jones for his opinion, he agreed that it should be published. He commented, "It gives a clear picture of what people thought and think about Treutlen, and I find that very interesting. The conflicting stories about Treutlen's death show how oral history functions."

During the greater part of his life, Treutlen lived in the Parish of St. Matthew, usually written St. Matthew's Parish, Georgia. In the fall of 1778, the British captured Savannah and began moving inland along the Savannah River. When they reached Ebenezer, Treutlen fled to St. Matthews [sic] Parish, South Carolina. He was sent by St. Matthew's Parish to the Georgia House of Assembly; and, when elected to the South Carolina Assembly from St. Matthews, South Carolina, he did not serve.

Treutlen's political life is better documented than his private life. This void of information about his personal existence has been filled with contradictory rumors.

This work contains a number of conflicting rumors with no attempt to favor one over another. Each reader can judge which rumor, if any, is believable. The scarcity of documented material coupled with the abundance of rumors led to the selection of a title for this work.

The Historic Effingham Society and I thank Rebecca Heidt for her faithful and diligent work as typographer.

Edna Q. Morgan
June 12, 1998

John Adam Treutlen, the First Constitutional
Governor of the State of Georgia.

John Adam Treutlen, the first Constitutional Governor of Georgia, has been called one of Effingham County's heroes, a staunch Salzburger, a Revolutionary Patriot (Rebah Mallory), Mystery Man (Harrell), A Forgotten Patriot (Griffin), and Patriot in Oblivion (Suddeth). Why these last three epithets?

For many years, Georgia historians paid little attention to Treutlen. When interest did appear, it was discovered that his political life is better documented than his private life, which contains more legends than facts. There are more questions than definite answers. When and where was he born? How did he spend his time before becoming prominent? What did he do after leaving office as governor? If he were murdered, by whom was it done, when and where? Where is he buried? These questions have conflicting answers.

Where and when was John Adam Treutlen born? No one knows. A bust in the rotunda of the Georgia State Capitol is identified as "John Adam Treutlen 1726-1782 Salzburg Patriot." It further states that he was born in Berchtesgaten, Austria, and was a member of the Salzburger settlement at Ebenezer. The same date and country of birth are given in *Backtracking in Barbour Co., Alabama*, and also by Dr. James F. Cook. Judge Richard H. Clark writes about a tradition among some Treutlen descendants that he was a native of England. Ruth Suddeth mentions that "1733 is the generally accepted date for Treutlen's birth, though some place it years earlier." She gives his birthplace as either Austria or "the town of Gosport, England, during the prolonged stay the Treutlen family made in that country." Most sources say that pirates attacked the ship on which the Treutlens were sailing to America; the father was imprisoned and died; and the mother and sons left to find their way to America as best they could. No dates are given for the initial sailing or the arrival. Jones gives a better account of the Treutlens' trip to Georgia.

The Treutlens and other Salzburgers, who had fled their homeland to avoid religious persecution, had started to America on the *Two Brothers*. This vessel was captured by two Spanish corsairs (pirate ships) and taken to Bilboa, Spain, where they were robbed and imprisoned. Mr. Treutlen died in prison, but his wife, Maria Clara, and her three sons were sent with the other captives to Gosport, England, on a cartel (prisoner exchange) ship. A few wealthy passengers were able to secure enough funds to return to their former homes.

While the Treutlens and others were stranded in England on the charity of the townsfolk, the oldest Treutlen son, Christian, was apprenticed to John Carver. This apprenticeship furnished Mrs. Treutlen with some funds to help her care for herself and her two younger sons, John Adam and Frederick. Finally the Trustees engaged a hundred of the survivors of the ill-fated *Two Brothers* as servants and put them onboard the *Judith* captained by Walter Quarme for a second trip toward America. Shortly after Mrs. Treutlen and her younger sons set sail, Christian Treutlen and John Carver were drowned in Gosport Harbor.

For a while it seemed as if this group of Salzburgers was destined not to reach Georgia. Jones says the *Judith* also had difficulties. Some passengers, crew members, and the captain became ill with fever, and the captain died. The first mate, who was near death, was unable to take charge. "The ship might never have reached Frederica if a passenger named Bartholomaus Zouberbuhler, a landlubber ... had not known enough geometry to plot the ship's course with the help of an illiterate sailor." (Jones, 88) The *Judith* arrived early in 1746. Another passenger aboard this ship was the Reverend Herman Lemke, who was selected to assist Pastor Boltzius at Jerusalem Church, Ebenezer, after the death of the Reverend Gronau.

Frederick Treutlen secured a grant of land between Savannah and Ebenezer, married and settled there, but John Adam and his mother went to Vernonburg, where she remarried. In order to secure an education for her son and remove him from his stepfather's influence, Treutlen's mother took him to Ebenezer. Finck says, "In 1747, at the age of fourteen years, the young son (John Adam) at Ebenezer was confirmed." The pastors at Ebenezer were accomplished scholars, and they laid the foundation for John Adam's broad education. In his reports Boltzius frequently "commends him for his industry at work, his zeal in learning, and his obedience in conduct." (Finck, 180) "How vigorously the studious young Treutlen mastered English composition is revealed in the strong prose of his eleven forceful proclamations as governor." (Suddeth, 16)

Early Career

John Adam's early career was varied. He taught school at Ebenezer. (Suddeth, 16) He was a "surveyor of roads." (Quick) He worked on a plantation for a while. Then, he went to live in the home of the surgeon of the colony, Dr. Mayer.

When Dr. Mayer and the two pastors noted a change in John Adam after visiting his mother, they realized it was caused by the evil influence of his stepfather. The three older men set the young boy straight, and he "became very respectful to his employer, grateful to the two pastors, and very devout in the performance of his religious duties." (Finck, 181) He served for a year as a store clerk in Savannah, "which added both to his experience and knowledge and taught him tact and grace in dealing with people." (Finck, 181) According to the plaque in the Georgia Hall of Fame, Treutlen was a colonel of the Effingham County Militia.

After his marriage, about 1756, to Marguerite Dupuis, an orphan from Purysburg, South Carolina, who had been educated at Ebenezer, John Adam settled on his own land in the vicinity of Sister's Ferry and became a planter. He and Marguerite had eight children, named: Christiana, Jonathan, Elizabeth, Dorothea,

Mary, Hannah, Christian, and John. Marguerite died while Treutlen was governor. (Cook, 16)

When Treutlen began acquiring land for a plantation, he also began raising cattle as food for his household as well as for a source of cash. To identify his cattle, he developed a cattle brand which he recorded at the court house. This brand, or symbol, was also used to mark other personal property. An amateur archaeologist, a friend of the present owners of a part of Treutlen's estate, has unearthed a solid German silver serving spoon marked with this symbol, shown on page 10.

As a plantation owner, Treutlen had extensive acreage. Estimates of his holdings differ. Suddeth (19) says that by 1760, he had a plantation of 12,000 acres and 23 slaves. However, Finck claims that Treutlen owned over 13,000 acres. Records in the Georgia archives show that between 1757 and 1771, Treutlen was granted a total of 1,443 acres in St. Matthew's Parish and 600 acres in St. Phillip's Parish. South Carolina archives contain records of a 70-acre grant to Treutlen, and also deeds to 425 purchased acres, all bordering the Savannah River in St. Peters Parish, Granville County, approximately opposite his Georgia property. (A copy of the original plat and deed is on pages 8 and 9).

How much land Treutlen bought or sold is uncertain. On June 12, 1767, Treutlen bought 200 acres from Balthesar Reiser and sold it to Daniel Zettler on December 4, 1773. Treutlen also bought 450 acres on Cowpen Branch from Jacob Metzger on June 4, 1773, and left it in his will to his daughter, Mary. One interesting transaction has been uncovered. Treutlen was granted 50 acres bordering the Savannah River in 1767 and had it resurveyed in July 1769. The surveyor's plat, shown on page 7, is unusual for that time because it shows a large house on the land. Perhaps Treutlen, his wife, and five children were living there in 1769. (Jonathan had died in 1758 and Christiana in 1759, and

MAP OF TREUTLEN'S LAND

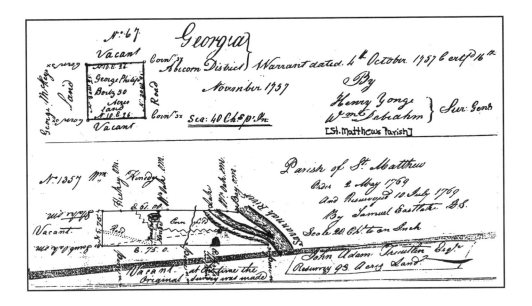

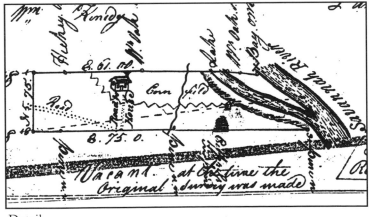

Detail

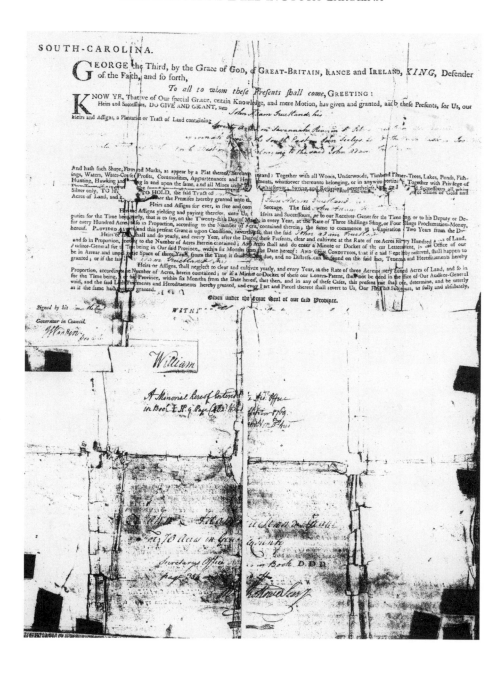

Plat Accompanying
Treutlen's Land Deed in South Carolina

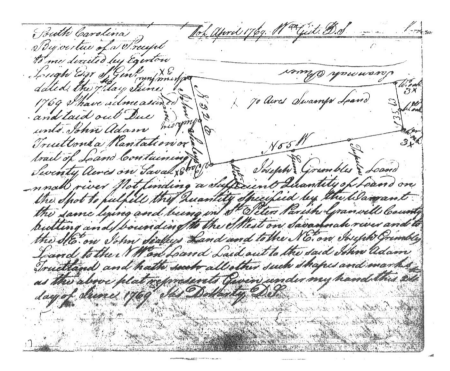

A picture of the German silver serving spoon which was unearthed at Treutlen's homesite. The spoon measures 8 inches (20.5 cm) long including its bowl which measures 3 inches (7.4 cm) long by 1⅝ inches (2.2 cm) wide. Also pictured is Treutlen's brand.

John had not been born.) Treutlen may have been preparing to move. Maybe his home in the "red brick field" had been completed. Whatever his reason for the survey may have been, Treutlen learned or verified that the parcel of land that he believed to be 50 acres actually measured 93 acres. Treutlen sold 50 acres of the granted parcel to Abr. de Roche on December 19, 1769. Treutlen then applied for and received a grant, on February 6, 1790, for the additional 43 acres which he had already cleared and begun to use.

In his will John Adam Treutlen divided his land among his children. William Kennedy, as husband of Elizabeth Treutlen, received her share from Christian Treutlen, the executor of the estate. The plat shown on pages 12 and 13 indicate how William Kennedy's estate was divided among his children: Benjamin; Mary, wife of Seth Daniels; and Catherine, with Benjamin as trustee for her because she was unmarried at the time of her father's death. This plat includes the area known today as the "red brick field."

Although John Adam Treutlen was a prosperous and busy planter, he was not too busy to become involved in the religious life of the community. In 1765, he was elected a deacon in the Jerusalem Lutheran Church at Ebenezer and continued to hold this position until his death. He was the leading officer of the congregation when Muhlenberg, the leading Lutheran patriarch in America at that time, came to Ebenezer in 1774. Treutlen "made a most favorable impression upon Muhlenberg by his calm, deliberate, wise, and peace-seeking manner of procedure; by his conscientious and unwavering defense of the right; and by his consistent Christian character and conduct." (Finck, 181)

Muhlenberg and Treutlen had been corresponding with one another for several years. When Muhlenberg was looking for a home and work for his seventeen year old nephew, Ismael, to

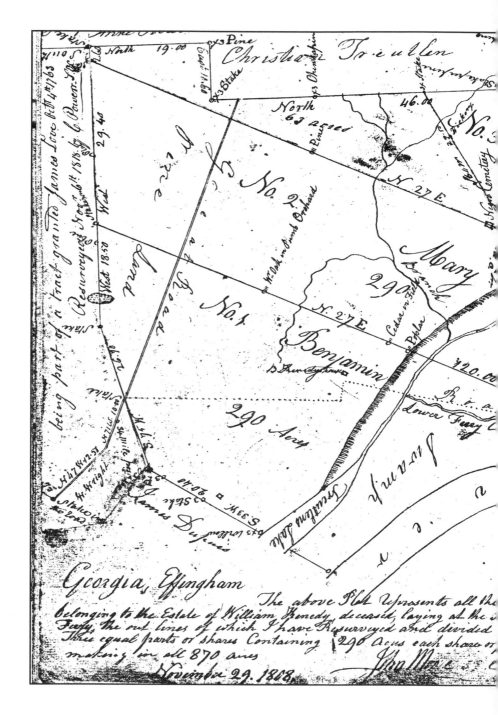

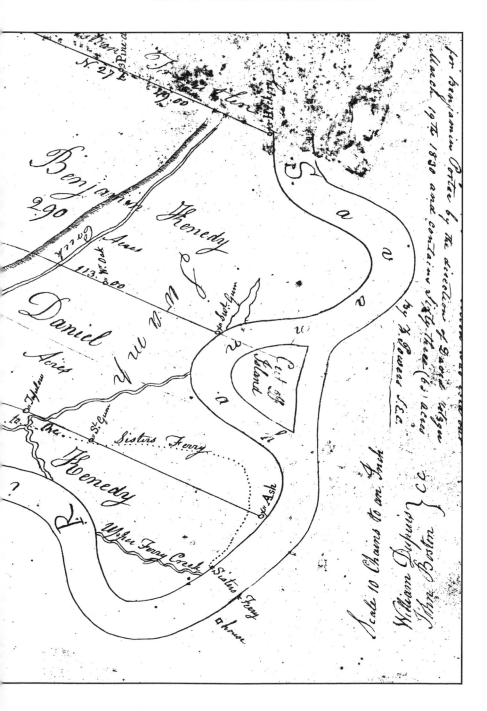

remove him from the influence of his stepfather, he sent him to live with the Treutlens, who became like parents to him. Ismael and one of Treutlen's daughters became fond of one another, and it was rumored that they would be married by Muhlenberg when he visited Ebenezer. The wedding never took place because two months before the visit, Ismael was killed by a spirited horse he was trying to control. Muhlenberg and Treutlen continued their friendship and correspondence. When Treutlen's wife died, Muhlenberg wrote him a letter contrasting "the joy of May 8th with the sorrow of June 25th." This letter was in response to Treutlen's letter telling Muhlenberg of his election as governor and of Marguerite's death. (Finck, 183-84)

In Politics

John Adam Treutlen also became politically active. While serving as a magistrate, he was sent by St. Matthew's Parish to the
Provincial Assembly under the British Governor Wright. (Finck,
184) He served three terms in the Common House of Assembly.
He was one of the thirty-six men who served in both the royal
and the Revolutionary legislatures. He was appointed a member
of the Council of Safety created by the assembly to serve during
the intermission. "In the work of this committee he was in the
van of activity. The British Governor was arrested [in January
1776] and held a prisoner on their order." (Finck, 184)

"He (Treutlen) participated in the fiery meetings at Tondee's
Tavern in Savannah where Georgians debated the 'political phi-
losophy of the Revolution which was fast becoming common
speech from the St. Mary's to the Androscoggin.'" (Suddeth, 17)
When the Revolutionary War began, the congregation of Jerusalem Church was divided. There were many Tories. Treutlen,
however, remained loyal to his adopted country. (Griffin, 892)

In 1776, a temporary constitution for Georgia was adopted
with Button Gwinnett as provisional governor. On February 5,

1777, a formal constitution was adopted. This constitution had several provisions. In order to disestablish the Church of England, the old parishes were displaced by counties. Georgia was divided into eight counties: "Chatham, Glynn, Effingham, Richmond, Burke, Liberty, Camden, and Wilkes." (Cook, 16) Treutlen's home parish, St. Matthew's, now became Effingham County.

The constitution did not go into effect entirely until May when John Adam Treutlen was elected by the Assembly as Georgia's first governor. "During the three months intervening, Button Gwinnett acted as governor pro-tem." (Atlanta Journal, 8) Treutlen had served with Button Gwinnett and five others on the committee that wrote the Constitution of 1777. (Cook, 16)

Gwinnett-McIntosh Duel

These were troubled times and Treutlen faced many conflicts.
As the incumbent, Gwinnett had expected to become governor,
but was disappointed. Also, the assembly began an investigation
of Gwinnett's invasion of Florida in April 1777, while he was
acting governor. He had used his authority to interfere with General McIntosh's planned attack, with his continental troops, on
the British at St. Augustine. At the conclusion of the investigation, upholding Gwinnett, McIntosh, who "was incensed not only
by the criticism of his military leadership and Gwinnett's inter-
ference, but also by the arrest of his brother, George, on suspicion of treason," called Gwinnett a "scoundrel and a lying ras-
cal." (Cook, 15) In the ensuing duel which took place, on May 26,
1777, in Governor Wright's meadow outside Savannah, both men
were wounded in the leg. According to Rutherford, the reason
they were both shot in the leg was that "both were good enough
shots to hit the other, and both were gentlemen enough to aim
below the knee." Other sources refute this claim that both men
aimed below the knee, saying that Gwinnett, who was wounded
in the thigh, died three days later from gangrene.

After Gwinnett's death, the wounded Lachlan McIntosh went into hiding. Governor Treutlen made plans to conduct McIntosh, one of his former supporters, to Philadelphia. However, General McIntosh ordered Colonel Joseph Habersham to arrest the conductors on the day set for the journey. Five hundred Georgians signed a letter to Treutlen asking for McIntosh to be removed from Georgia. (Quick)

On June 18, 1777, Treutlen wrote to John Hancock telling him of the events leading to the duel and mentioning that on the East Florida campaign, General McIntosh and his officers refused to attend Councils of War with officers of the Georgia Militia. Treutlen, as well as Gwinnett, thought the military should be subservient to the Civil Authority. Treutlen also told Hancock of McIntosh's ploy to delay his arrest. He informed Hancock that he was sending McIntosh to Philadelphia under proper guard, commanded by Lieutenant Colonel Ferrell because the Georgia House of Assembly thought that Congress, not biased by any motives, would form an impartial and just judgement of McIntosh's conduct. On October 4, 1777, Congress decided to send McIntosh to Valley Forge.

OTHER PROBLEMS AS GOVERNOR

Meanwhile Treutlen was confronted by another problem which had been fermenting for several months. His supporters expected him to advance the cause of statehood, but his ability to do so was tested immediately. Earlier in the year, William H. Drayton had brought an official proposal from South Carolina for Georgia to become part of that state. (Harrell) Drayton presented elaborate arguments as to why the two states should join. He claimed that "union would end existing jealousy, improve trade, raise land prices, and make Savannah a great port." (Cook, 16)

In January 1777, Drayton first presented South Carolina's proposal to the Georgia Convention meeting in Savannah. Although it was "bitterly opposed by Treutlen, Gwinnett, and Noble W. Jones" (Quick) and was rejected by the convention, Drayton stayed in Georgia trying to gain support for the proposal. Griffin (892) says that "many financiers were persuaded to favor the scheme." Drayton continued to cause dissension among Georgia leaders. After the Gwinnett-McIntosh duel, Drayton "heaped odium upon Treutlen and his Council, charging that they had done an injustice to McIntosh and were Tories in disguise." (Quick)

In July 1777, Drayton threatened that if Georgia did not accept the plan, South Carolina would build a city opposite Savannah and attempt to ruin that city. Upon the hearing of this threat, Treutlen was so angered that he pounded his desk and ordered the arrest of Drayton and his associates. (Quick) With the consent of the Executive Council, Treutlen issued a proclamation. It begins

> "GEORGIA
> By his Honour John Adam Treutlen,
> Esquire, Captain-General, Governor, and
> Commander-in-Chief in and over the
> said state,
>
> a Proclamation
> Whereas it hath been..." (Caldwell, 320)
> Caldwell quotes the entire proclamation
> showing that "one hundred pounds, law-
> ful money of the said State" was offered
> for the arrest. The proclamation ends
> thus:
>
> "Given under my Hand and Seal in
> the council chamber at Savannah, this fif-
> teenth day of July, one thousand seven
> hundred and seventy-seven.
>
> John Adam Treutlen
> By His Honour's Command,
> James Whitfield, Secretary,
> GOD SAVE THE CONGRESS."
> (Caldwell, 321)

Drayton was made aware of Treutlen's feelings and crossed the River to South Carolina before he could be arrested. (Harrell)

As governor under the constitution, Treutlen could serve only one year without reelection. He could not veto legislation, act without consent of the Executive Council, or address the Assembly in person. The Assembly had 72 members, 12 of whom were selected to become the Executive Council. (Cook, 16) Members of Treutlen's Council were: "Jonathan Bryan, John Houstoun, Thomas Chisholm, William Holzendorf, John Fulton, John Jones, John Walton, William Few, Arthur Fort, John Coleman, Benjamin Andrews and William Peacock." (Caldwell, 320) On two occasions during military danger, the Executive Council requested Governor Treutlen to take the whole executive power until the danger passed. (Cook, 16)

One of these times of military danger was when "he directed an expedition against the British at Frederica, which was captured along with two warships and some supplies of war." (Suddeth, 17) Another time was in one of the Indian outbreaks on the Georgia frontier when "he took his place at the head of the militia and drove back the enemy to their great confusion and disaster, and we do not hear of their returning again." (Finck, 185)

Treutlen had to contend not only with the British, the Indians, and the "Combiners" as Drayton and his associates were called; he also had to deal with Tories within the state. "Governor Treutlen was so aggressive in his campaign against the Tories and the British that it is recorded that, of all men in the country, he was most hated by them. They singled him out for vindictive harassment and placed a price on his head." (Suddeth, 892)

As Governor, Treutlen had to deal with financial problems. At the beginning of his governorship, the state was able to pay for its own defense. As time passed, the expenses of the government and the Revolution became too much for the state to handle. Treutlen mortgaged his personal property to help defray the state's expenses. Years later his son, Christian, paid off the mortgage. (Suddeth, 17) Finally Treutlen appealed to the Continental Congress for help. "To keep Georgia's troops in the field

Congress voted $400,000 to redeem Georgia's bills of credit and $300, 000 for future expenses." (Cook, 16)

In reporting on Treutlen's service to Georgia, Finck (181) states: "They (the British) were foiled in their attempt to hold the port of Savannah by the gallant services of men like Governor John Adam Treutlen, the greatest Lutheran layman produced by the Salzburgers in Georgia." Finck (185) says: "His term of service was marked by bravery and brilliancy. He issued eleven masterful proclamations with telling effect."

When Treutlen completed his term as governor, he returned to his plantation, and on January 14, 1778, he married a widow, Mrs. Annie Unselt. (Cook, 16) However, in 1779, Treutlen, who knew that the British had branded him a "rebel governor" and put him under the unalterable ban of death, fled with his family to Orangeburg District, South Carolina, when the British recaptured Savannah and began devastating the state as far north as Augusta. During this devastation, the English troops reportedly burned Treutlen's houses and barns to the ground and confiscated his property. (Suddeth, 17).

British Occupy Treutlen's Plantation

The leader of the British troops who confiscated Treutlen's property was Lieutenant Colonel Archibald Campbell, who seemed to be more practical than vindictive. Torching the property was not a priority when he arrived at the plantation on January 4, 1779. On the contrary, he used it as a post to help secure command of the Savannah River.

In his journal, Campbell tells that he and his troops left Ebenezer in search of the Rebel army and soon reached Treutlen's, which he spells Troitland's, plantation about nine miles away. (See maps on pages 24 and 25 showing both sides of the Savannah River.) At the Treutlen plantation, Campbell learned that the Rebels, as well as the Treutlen family, had recently crossed the river at a neighboring ferry known as Two Sisters. How the location was named remains in question. Some say that two sisters drowned while crossing the river at this point. Others claim it was named because of the two bluffs between which it is located. The exact location of Sister's Ferry today may differ from that in Treutlen's time. This question arises because Lieutenant Colonel Archibald Campbell's map, prepared while in the

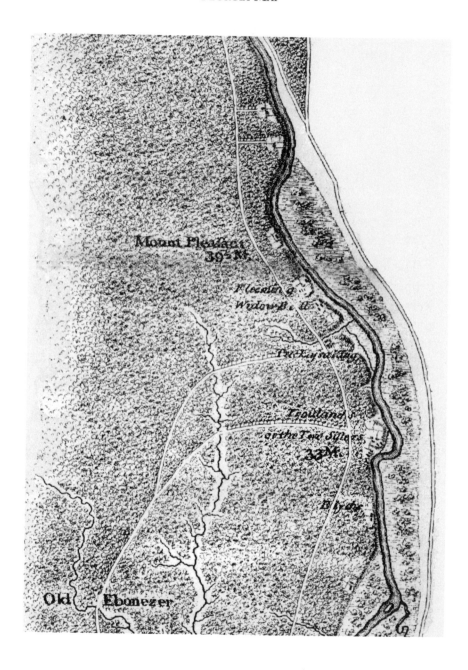

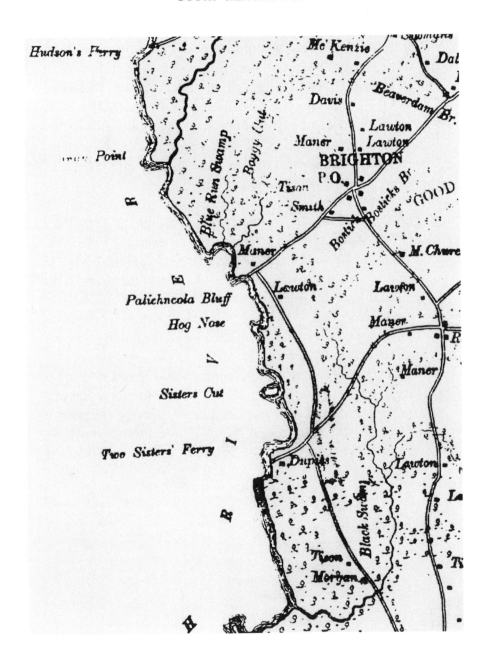

area, indicates a site north of the present day location of Sister's Ferry present day location.

Campbell improved the military position of the plantation by "shutting up the avenues between the Houses, and opening Loop Holes in all the Buildings that could afford any Degree of Defence [sic]." Leaving the York Volunteers to guard this post, Campbell and the rest of his troops searched unsuccessfully for Rebels from there to Hudson's Ferry, where they spent the night. Returning the ten miles to Treutlen's plantation, Campbell stayed there overnight before continuing to Ebenezer.

A few weeks later when Campbell began his march to capture Augusta, he and his troops spent their first night at Treutlen's plantation. Also, during his retreat from Augusta in February, Campbell sent Colonel Turnbull with the York Volunteers ahead to Treutlen's place when he heard that General Lincoln with his Continental Army was planning to come across the Savannah River at Sister's Ferry. A few days later, Campbell stopped at the plantation to see that everything was secure and the enemy had not crossed there into Georgia.

When Campbell gave his final report to General Prevost before leaving Georgia in March 1779, he recommended that 600 troops be placed at Treutlen's plantation to prevent the enemy from crossing the river there. Thus, it seems that Treutlen's home was burned only when it was no longer a useful post for the British troops.

TREUTLEN IN SOUTH CAROLINA

Meanwhile, John Adam Treutlen and his family were safely across the Savannah River. Some sources say the Treutlens went to stay with relatives in South Carolina. Others say he and his family moved into a blockhouse — a strong wooden fort with a projecting second story and openings in the walls for the defenders to shoot from. From South Carolina, Treutlen continued to fight for the freedom of his country. "His name is found enrolled among the soldiers of the continental line, and it is believed that he may have served as a volunteer under General Anthony Wayne." (Suddeth, 17, 18)

Treutlen's political activity continued. Anderson writes, "...he also was at one time a legislator in South Carolina. He was one of the representatives from St. Matthews Parish and Orange Parish, South Carolina, elected in 1781, to the Jacksonboro Assembly under Governor Rutledge." Contrary to this statement, Finck says, "...he was elected to the State (South Carolina) Assembly from his district, but circumstances prevented him from serving." The circumstances were that Treutlen had also been elected to the Georgia Assembly, which was meeting in Augusta. Since that city had been freed again from British control, it had been named the capital of Georgia. Treutlen took an active part in all the business and served on some important committees. "The Assembly adjourned January 12th to meet again July 1st, but the governor called a special session to meet April 18." (Finck, 186)

When the roll was called for this meeting, Treutlen did not respond as he was not present. "The Assembly records give us the information that a certain one was appointed on a committee in the room (place) of Mr. Treutlen, deceased." (Finck, 186)

TREUTLEN'S DEATH

There are several accounts of Treutlen's death. No one knows the exact date, but all agree it took place between January 12 and April 18, 1782. Finck (186) writes that it was reported to Muhlenberg that Treutlen had been decoyed from his South Carolina home by four or five Tories and "barbarously murdered."

On the other hand, Quick asks, "Did a revengeful McIntosh have something to do with Treutlen's death?" Quick agrees that Treutlen was lured from his home and killed; but since he had experience as a soldier and statesman, Quick doubts if Treutlen would have been lured from home by anyone unknown to him.

Suddeth (17) also suggests that the culprits may not have been Tories. She writes that accusations made against Treutlen by Drayton have "...led to the suspicion, held by a few, that Drayton's followers may have had a part a few years later in the death of Treutlen."

Yet another theory as to the identity of Treutlen's murderer or murderers is advanced by Dr. George Fenwick Jones, a historian who knew that the Tories were not active in Orangeburg County at the time of Treutlen's death. Jones (129) suggests that perhaps Treutlen had been murdered by a personal enemy, maybe a jilted suitor, since he had recently married his third wife.

Another version of Treutlen's death is given by Jacob C. Waldhour, who writes that Treutlen and his family had moved to Carolina; and, after the death of Treutlen's second wife, he married for a third time in 1782. Eight days after this marriage, eight Tories or refugees went to Treutlen's house and told him to come out. When he refused, they began to set fire to the house, so he came out. They took him a short distance away, killed him, and "cut him to pieces with the sword. His children moved back here. ...Two of his daughters are married, one lives in Goshen, the other in Purisburg [sic], and they have their brothers and sisters with them." No mention is made of the third wife's name or what became of her.

There are other conflicting stories of how Treutlen was murdered. Suddeth reports two of these versions. "A relatively mild version states that Treutlen was dragged to his death by being tied to a spirited horse which was made to dash off at high speed..." She also says that Lawton B. Evans in his *History of Georgia*, first published in 1898, over a hundred years after Treutlen's death, states that Treutlen was deceived by the British and Tories asking for food. When Treutlen unbarred the door, they seized him and took him outside where he was "drawn and quartered." Another version, given by Clark, states, "...(He) was murdered in the most horrible manner. He was tied to a tree and hacked to pieces with swords in the presence of his family."

"Dr. A.S. Salley, former state historian of South Carolina, is one who believes the murder mystery about Governor Treutlen is a myth that needs to be exploded..." (Suddeth, 18) In a letter dated June 10, 1953, Dr. Salley expresses his views. He doubts that Treutlen was murdered because the resolutions adopted by the Georgia Assembly are in the language usually used for those who died a natural death. Also, the British troops in South Carolina were confined to Charleston at that time. The two pro-British newspapers, whose files Salley researched, contained no boast of killing this "enemy of his Majesty." The numerous British accounts of the war in South Carolina do not mention the capture or execution of Treutlen. (Suddeth, 18)

Perhaps Salley could find no mention of Treutlen's death in South Carolina because he was not killed there. Maybe, just maybe, the account handed down in the Metzger family of Clyo, Georgia, could be a correct version. Betty Graham, an Effingham County native, has written down a legend told to her by her grandmother, Kate Metzger Maner, who heard it from her grandfather, Moses Metzger.

Moses's father, David, lived with his parents near Sister's Ferry just down the road from the Treutlens. One night, in 1782, seventeen-year-old David heard a scream and went to investigate. Mrs. Treutlen told him that three men had come to ask Treutlen about some money he was said to be safekeeping for the state. He went outside to talk to them, and they went behind the house. Some time later when the men returned to the front of the house, they told Mrs. Treutlen that "if she wanted her husband, she could find him cut up on the wood pile." No money was ever found. Treutlen was buried at night for fear that the men might dig him up to see if the money had been buried with him.

This writer finds a slight flaw in the Metzger version of the murder. It is true that the Metzger home was just down the road from the Treutlen home near Sister's Ferry. However, if all Treutlen's houses and barns had been burned to the ground three years earlier as had been previously reported, had Treutlen rebuilt a home during the war? If Treutlen had moved back to Georgia, why was he elected to the South Carolina legislature? On the other hand, he had attended the meetings of the Georgia

Assembly which had adjourned in Augusta on January 12, 1782. He may have come down the Augusta Road to inspect his Georgia property, now freed from the British, before returning to South Carolina. Instead of being burned to the ground, the house still may have been habitable, and he and his family decided to linger there a few days. The men who were seeking the money could have followed him from Augusta. Of course, these are just more questions and speculation.

There is also a tradition of how Governor Treutlen's murder was avenged after the war ended. According to Griffin (893), while Treutlen's daughter, Mary, and her brother were guests in the South Carolina home of Colonel Rumph, Mary recognized her father's watch being worn by another guest. Mary told her brother about the watch. He and his friends confronted the young man, who confessed that he had been one of the Tories who killed Treutlen, and he named others. The guilty men were all hanged from the limbs of the oak tree where Treutlen was murdered.

SEARCH FOR GRAVESITE

Most accounts of Treutlen's death end by saying his gravesite
is unknown. Suddeth tells of an official search being made on
February 6, 1931 by the Salzburger Society. This search was based
on information related many years ago by a former slave, "Skip"
Ryals, who lived to be 102 years old. Before being granted his
freedom in 1806, "Skip" had belonged to Arthur Ryall, Jr., a plantation owner at Tuckasee King. According to R.B. Mallory, Sr.,
"Skip" related that his "Ole' Massa" told him that the people
from South Carolina came to Governor Treutlen's mansion in
the Red Brick Field, murdered him, cut up his body, and buried it
in the garden back of his house. Later Treutlen's son carried his
body down to the Mill Branch, which is about ¼ mile away toward Kennedy's Lake. The spot has been pointed out from one
generation to another. Otto Gnann writes that his father, Alvin
Gnann, took part in the search mentioned by Suddeth. He says
that two other members of the search party were George Metzger,
one of David Metzger's descendants, and Dr. Lynn, a Lutheran
minister from Savannah, who was archivist of the Lutheran Synod
of Georgia.

Reports of this search, told by Suddeth and Gnann, indicate that someone had dug in that spot because the soil was a mixture of clay and sandy loam. Also the searchers reported they saw the outline of a coffin. Some rusty nails, buttons, and something that may have been bone were taken from the spot, wrapped in a cloth and taken by Dr. Lynn to Savannah. The Effingham men never saw them again. Dr. Lynn died a short time later, and it is believed that these artifacts probably were discarded.

Several years later, Otto Gnann asked his father to show him the spot. He called George Metzger to lead them to it. Otto Gnann writes, "It is on a mound at the foot of a Laurel or Magnolia tree near the Savannah River. I don't remember which kind of tree."

For over a century, nothing was done to pay tribute to this First Governor of the State of Georgia. Caldwell (322) suggests that Treutlen's burial place may have been forgotten because of the troubles of the time. The Revolutionary War was still in progress, and, after the war, Treutlen had no descendants in public life in Georgia to keep his memory alive.

Harrell quotes historian Lucian Lamar Knight, who writes, "His memory has become entangled with the weeds and briars of neglect."

MEMORIALS

In Judge Clark's memoirs, written many years before their publication in 1931, he says that the state owes some recognition to Treutlen because all governors since the Revolution "owe their official position and reputation" to the Revolutionary governors. In 1917, the state did recognize Treutlen by naming a county in middle Georgia for him.

In South Carolina a monument to Treutlen was erected in 1914, by the William Thompson and Emily Geiger Chapters of the Daughters of the American Revolution of St. Matthews, South Carolina. This marker is said to be near the spot where Treutlen was murdered at Metts Crossing. Mary Douglass says that the marker is on the lawn of a two story house about 7 miles from St. Matthews, at the intersection of Highways No. 6 and No. 176.

A copy of a portrait of Governor Treutlen, once owned by his great-grandson, John F. Treutlen, is in the Calhoun County Historical Commission Library in St. Matthews. Griffin (893) says that the portrait's inscription lists Treutlen's accomplishments. A Treutlen descendant, Mrs. Frank Petry of Eufaula, Alabama, has a portrait of Treutlen in his colonial blue uniform. (Hill, 109)

Mrs. Hill also quotes a description of Treutlen taken from page 198 of Sophia Foster's "Revolutionary Reader."

> "He had a military bearing
> — profuse stock of hair futilely bom-
> barding an obstinate cowlick, large
> piercing (blue) eyes fringed by
> shaggy brows with a drooping lid,
> nose Roman, a bold intellectual fore-
> head, marked cheek bones with a face
> — sharp angular chin, thin lips
> closely plastered together. Altogether
> not a man to take liberties with."

When Georgia was celebrating its Bicentennial in 1933, R.B. Mallory sent a tree from Treutlen's land to be planted in Governor Treutlen's honor in Bicentennial Memorial Forest near Atlanta. In 1938, Rebah Mallory sent another relic, a brick, from Treutlen's property near Sister's Ferry to the Museum at the State Capitol. This brick was handmade and almost perfect with just a few chipped places. This brick, larger and heavier than our modern ones, had been given to her by Caesar Metzger, another of David Metzger's descendants, who had plowed it up from Treutlen's home site.

A marble bust of Governor John Adam Treutlen is now in the Georgia Hall of Fame in the rotunda of the Georgia Capitol. This bust, along with busts of Archibald Bulloch, George M. Troupe, Benjamin Hawkins, and Peter Early, was unveiled on March 19, 1960. These and eight previously installed busts — Button Gwinnett, Alexander Hamilton Stephens, Lyman Hall, George Walton, William Few, Abraham Baldwin, William H. Crawford, and Crawford W. Long, M.D. — were commissioned to be done by Bryant Baker, an English-born New York sculptor. Mr. Baker was in Atlanta to see to the proper placing and lighting of the busts. (Daniel)

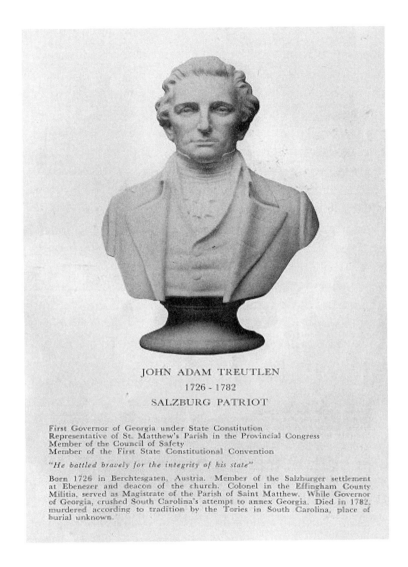

JOHN ADAM TREUTLEN
1726 - 1782

SALZBURG PATRIOT

First Governor of Georgia under State Constitution
Representative of St. Matthew's Parish in the Provincial Congress
Member of the Council of Safety
Member of the First State Constitutional Convention

"He battled bravely for the integrity of his state"

Born 1726 in Berchtesgaten, Austria. Member of the Salzburger settlement
at Ebenezer and deacon of the church. Colonel in the Effingham County
Militia, served as Magistrate of the Parish of Saint Matthew. While Governor
of Georgia, crushed South Carolina's attempt to annex Georgia. Died in 1782,
murdered according to tradition by the Tories in South Carolina, place of
burial unknown.

A scanned image of page 11 of "The Hall of Fame for Illustrious Georgians" at the State Capitol in Atlanta, Georgia on Saturday, March 19, 1960.

About the same time that Treutlen was being inducted into the Georgia Hall of Fame, the Georgia Salzburger Society was working toward having the newly completed bridge linking South Carolina to Georgia at Tuckasee King named the John Adam Treutlen Bridge. Plans for a marker to be placed on the Georgia side of the bridge were formulated. Martha Anderson suggests that the bridge would be a fitting way for the two states to share a memorial to a man who was a leader in both states. Nevertheless, this project failed because South Carolina prefers to name bridges in honor of living people.

However, the idea of a monument to Treutlen persisted, and the afternoon program of the Georgia Salzburger Society on Labor Day, September 2, 1963, was devoted to the unveiling of a five foot monument to John Adam Treutlen. This monument at Jerusalem Lutheran Church, at Ebenezer Landing, Effingham County, was unveiled by Miss Rebah Mallory and G. Phillip Morgan, Jr., two of Governor John Adam Treutlen's descendants. (Rebah Mallory)

Although the bridge across the Savannah River connecting Effingham County, Georgia, and Jasper County, South Carolina, remains unnamed, Georgia Highway 119 which runs through Effingham, Liberty, Bryan, and Bulloch counties and ends at the bridge has been named the Governor John Adam Treutlen Highway. A resolution authorizing the State Department of Transportation to so designate it was adopted in the Georgia House on February 16, 1978, and in the Senate on March 1, 1978. A dedication ceremony was held in the Central Junior High School gym on March 20, 1978, by the school P.T.A.

On November 2, 1991, another dedication ceremony was held by the Historic Effingham Society. This ceremony included the unveiling of a marker on the shoulder of the highway on land formerly owned by Governor Treutlen at Tuckasee King.

Also, a framed picture of the governor was presented to the Society by Georgia State Representative Ann Purcell.

Although Governor Treutlen may have been forgotten for over a hundred years, his memory has been revived during the present century, and the above mentioned memorials will serve as reminders of his honorable and unselfish service to his parish, county, state, and country.

Griffin (893) mentions that a Coat of Arms, granted in 1571 by the Emperor of Austria to an ancestor of Governor Treutlen, contains this symbolism: "Generosity, peace and purity, military bravery, truth, and loyalty. John Adam Treutlen lived up to his heritage, casting glory on its image. Ironically, however, only the 'peace' seems to have eluded him."

A Coat of Arms for John Adam Treutlen may be just another rumor that has surfaced during the more than two hundred years since his death, adding another bit of glamour to his story. It is true that a Treutlen Coat of Arms does exist, but whether or not the person to whom it was granted was an ancestor of John Adam Treutlen is debatable until documented.

Serious researchers know that the Treutlens, like many others who came to America, were a poor family. The fact that John Adam Treutlen, who came to the Colony of Georgia as an indentured servant, rose above his humble beginnings to become the head of the State of Georgia, its first Constitutional Governor, is a tribute to his ability and industry.

Appendices

Treutlen's Proclamation

Georgia.

By his Honour John Adam Treutlen, Esquire, Captain-General, Governour, and Commander-in-Chief in and over the said State.

A Proclamation.

Whereas it hath been represented unto me, that William Henry Drayton, Esq., of the State of South Carolina, and divers other persons, whose names are yet unknown, are unlawfully endeavoring to poison the minds of the good people of this State against the Government thereof, and for that purpose are, by letters, petitions, and otherwise, daily exciting animosities among the inhabitants, under the pretence of redressing imaginary grievances, which by the said William Henry Drayton it is said this State labours under, the better to effect, under such specious pretences, an union between the states of Georgia and South Carolina, all of which are contrary to the Articles of Confederation, entered into, ratified, and confirmed by this State as a cement of union between the same and the other United and Independent States of America, and also against the resolution of the Convention of this State in that case made and entered into: Therefore, that such pernicious practices may be put to an end, and which, if not in due time prevented, may be of the most dangerous consequences, I have, by and with the advice and consent of the Executive Council of this State, thought fit to issue this Proclamation, hereby offering a reward of One Hundred Pounds, lawful money of the said State to be paid to any person or persons who shall apprehend the said William Henry Drayton, or any other person or persons aiding or abetting him in such unlawful practices, upon his or their conviction: And I do hereby strictly charge and require all magistrates and other persons to be vigilant and active in suppressing the same, and to take all lawful ways and means for the discovering and apprehending of such offender or offenders, so that he or they may be brought to condign punishment.

Given under my Hand and Seal in the Council Chamber at Savannah, this fifteenth day of July, one thousand seven hundred and seventy-seven.

JOHN ADAM TREUTLEN.

By His Honour's Command,
    JAMES WHITFIELD, Secretary
    GOD SAVE THE CONGRESS.

Appendix B

Governor John Adam Treutlen Highway Designated.
No. 232 (House Resolution No. 589-1710).

A Resolution

Authorizing and directing the State Department of Transportation to designate State Highway 119 as the "Governor John Adam Treutlen Highway"; and for other purposes.

Whereas, John Adam Treutlen was the first Governor of the State of Georgia and was an official member of the church of the Salzburgers at Ebenezer and was a citizen of that part of Effingham County which was then St. Matthew's Parish, and his home was about eight miles above Ebenezer, in the immediate neighborhood of Sister's Ferry; and

Whereas, he was a prominent figure among the Georgia patriots and was called to the chief magistracy of the State during the most eventful period of her history; and

Whereas, he took his place as a member of the Provincial Congress of 1775, among such men as Walton, Habersham, Bryant, Telfair, Houstoun, Clay, Cuthbert and McIntosh and was selected from among these as Governor of the new State; and

Whereas, John Adam Treutlen, first Governor of Georgia, was so brutally murdered by the Tories and was buried no one now living knows where; and

Whereas, Governor Treutlen, having in this sad way departed from the scene of action, and it being so long before the close of the war and having no son or other descendent in the State in public life, he was neglected and forgotten; and

Whereas, the State of Georgia has named a county after him; and

Whereas, a historical marker near Georgia 119 at Sister's Ferry, Clyo, Georgia, is erected.

Now, therefore, be it resolved by the General Assembly of Georgia, that the State Department of Transportation is hereby authorized to designate State Highway 119, which runs through the counties of Effingham, Bulloch, Bryan and Liberty, as the "Governor John Adam Treutlen Highway."

45

BE IT FURTHER RESOLVED that the State Department of Transportation is hereby authorized and directed to erect an appropriate plaque or sign at an appropriate location designating State Highway 119 as provided above.

BE IT FURTHER RESOLVED that the Clerk of the House of Representatives is hereby authorized and directed to transmit appropriate copies of this Resolution to the Honorable Tom Moreland, Commissioner of the State Department of Transportation, and to Central Junior High School in Springfield.

Approved April 6, 1978.

NOTES

Governor John Adam Treutlen issued the proclamation, shown as Appendix A, in response to a request made on the 14th of July, 1777, by the Council to offer a reward for the apprehension of Mr. Drayton and those associated with him.

The resolution, shown as Appendix B, can be found in the Local and Special Acts and Resolutions, Vol. II, page 4606, for the State of Georgia. This resolution was read and adopted in the House, February 10, 1978 and in the Senate, March 1, 1978. Presented by Rep. George Chance, 129th District, Pete Clifton, 107th District, Rep. Lane, 81st District, Rep. NeeSmith, 82nd District, and Senator Charles Wessels.

A computer-enhanced photocopy of a memorandum apparently penned and signed by John Adam Treutlen. The original copy of this memorandum is of unknown origin.

APPENDIX D
ARTIFACTS FOUND AT TREUTLEN'S HOMESITE

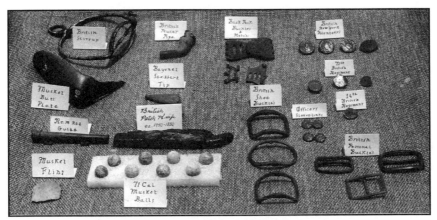

Top Photograph: Artifacts found on Governor Treutlen's land (top to bottom, left to right) include: British stirrup, musket butt plate, ramrod guide, musket flint, British pewter pipe, bayonet scabbard tip, British patch knife, 71st Calvary musket balls, backpack buckles and ketch, British shoe buckles, British New York Volunteers buttons, 71st British Regiment, 16th British Regiment, British personal buckles.
Bottom Photograph: Close-up of the buttons reveals more detail. These and other artifacts are on display at the Old Jail Museum in Springfield, Georgia.

About The Authors

Rebah Elizabeth Mallory
1902 - 1986

Rebah Elizabeth Mallory, a native of Clyo, Georgia, was born November 13, 1902, a daughter of Ransley Burge Mallory, who was born at Sister's Ferry, Georgia, and Ella (Pursley) Mallory; Ella was born at Americus, Georgia and moved to Guyton, Georgia with her family when she was a teenager. Rebah's father, known as "Mr. Rantz Mallory," was a great-great-great-grandson of John Adam Treutlen, an ancestry of which Rebah was very proud.

Rebah attended the Clyo schools, graduated from Savannah High School, and attend Brenau College, where she was a member of Tri Delta Sorority. After college she worked in her father's mercantile business for many years as a clerk and bookkeeper.

A lifelong member of the Clyo United Methodist Church, she served on the Official Board as church historian. She was a member of Clyo United Methodist Women, Clyo Homemakers Club, Georgia Salzburger Society, Brier Creek Chapter of The Daughters of the American Revolution, a charter member of Historic Effingham Society, and a member of Effingham County Committee for the National Bicentennial Celebration. As a member of this committee she wrote several articles for and participated in the proofreading of the *History of Effingham County, Georgia, 1733-1976.*

Miss Mallory was a charter member of the American Legion Auxiliary Post 209. During World War II, while her brothers were in service, she served as volunteer Chief Observer for the Clyo Post of the Aircraft Warning System with fifty other volunteers manning the post at R.B. Mallory's store in the daytime and the Clyo railroad depot at night from 1942-1945.

Rebah also took part in many county and local activities. She served as member and secretary of the Effingham County Library Board and publicity chairman for the Effingham County Hospital Auxiliary. She was the Clyo correspondent for the

Savannah Morning News. As Clyo correspondent for the *Spring-field Herald* for many years, she wrote a weekly column of "Clyo News," and when this newspaper published its Fiftieth Anniversary Edition, she was listed as a contributing editor.

Miss Mallory was instrumental in getting many of the historical markers placed in Effingham County. She wrote countless letters to Dr. John H. Goff, a member of the Georgia Historic Commission, suggesting sites that needed marking and seeking his aid to secure the markers.

One week after her eighty-fourth birthday, Rebah died quietly in her sleep on November 20, 1986. In all of her writing, Rebah's motto was, "If you can't say anything good about your community, don't say anything."

Edna Quinby Morgan

1913 -

Edna Gertrude Quinby was born October 22, 1913, in Charleston, South Carolina, a daughter of Bertrand A. and Lillie E. (Burn) Quinby, both of whom were Charleston natives. She graduated from Julian Mitchell School and Memminger High School before attending college. In 1935, she received an A.B. degree from the College of Charleston with majors in Latin and mathematics. In 1939, she received a M.A. degree from George Peabody College for Teachers with a major in education and minors in psychology and history. She has since taken graduate courses at Georgia Southern College.

On July 14, 1940, Edna and Hollis Albert Morgan were married in Charleston at the Church of the Holy Communion, of which she was a member and former Sunday School teacher. Hollis was the son of Arthur Ryal and Susan Gugie (Morgan) Morgan. The couple made their home near Clyo and became the parents of three children, Bertrand Ryal Morgan, Ashley Albert Morgan, and Sylvia Gertrude (Morgan) Hendrix. There are four grandsons and one granddaughter. After fifty-two years of marriage, Hollis died September 6, 1992.

Edna has been active in church, school, and community affairs. She organized the Clyo Girl Scout Troop after having been a First Class Scout and Scout Leader for several years in Charleston. She served as a member of the Effingham County Library Board. During World War II, she served with other teachers in the Clyo school in registering people in Clyo school district for gasoline and food ration stamps. In addition, she took some turns as a volunteer at Mallory's Store as an airplane spotter for the Aircraft Warning System. She has served as a P.T.A. officer, holding all offices except president.

Before her marriage, Edna taught for one year (1939-1940) in South Carolina, at Sullivan's Island. She taught thirty-one years in the Effingham County School System, eighteen years at Clyo

Consolidated High School (later named Clyo Elementary School), two years at Effingham County Junior High School, and eleven years at Effingham County High School, from which she retired in June, 1975. During her career she taught on every level from the first grade through the twelfth.

Edna is still taking an active part in community affairs. She is a member of Wingard Memorial Lutheran Church, being a former teacher and superintendent of the Sunday School, and treasurer and former president of the W.E.L.C.A. (formerly called L.C.W.). She is a member of the Clyo Homemakers Club, for which she has written a thirty year history. As an alumna of Peabody College, she joined the Alumni Association of Vanderbilt University when the two institutions merged. She also holds life membership in the following organizations: College of Charleston Alumni Association, Georgia Salzburger Society (Associate), Historic Effingham Society, Effingham Retired Teachers Association, and Georgia Retired Teachers Association. When the Georgia Retired Teachers Association asked members to send articles about their early teaching experiences for a bicentennial book, Edna was a contributor.

When the *History of Effingham County, Georgia, 1733-1976* was being planned, Rebah Mallory asked Edna to help her write an article about John Adam Treutlen and one about Tuckasee King for the book. After doing this, Edna compiled two more articles and assisted with typing and proofreading.

Edna enjoys going to meetings to keep abreast of what's happening, and to socialize with people who have similar interests. Therefore, she has recently joined the United Daughters of the Confederacy Effingham County Hussars Chapter No. 2285. She thanks the Lord that she is still able to take an active part in the community.

Cited Materials

List Of Resources
Partially Annotated

Since standard bibliographical form is not feasible using Rebah's collection, this writer decided to make the following divisions: books; magazines; clippings; photostatic copies of articles; printed programs; letters; additional handwritten or typed materials; and deeds, maps, and plats.

Books

Campbell, Colin, ed. *Journal of an Expedition against the Rebels of Georgia in North America Under the Orders of Archibald Campbell Esquire Lieut. Colol. of His Majesty's 71st Regimt.* 1778. Darien, Georgia: The Ashantilly Press, 1981.

Coulter, E. Merton. *Georgia A Short History.* Chapel Hill: The University of North Carolina Press, 1947.

Finck, William J. *Lutheran Landmarks and Pioneers in America.* Philadelphia: The United Lutheran Publication House, 1913.

Hill, Henrietta McCormick. *The Family Skeleton.* Montgomery, Alabama: The Paragon Press, Inc., 1958.

Jones, George Fenwick. *The Salzburger Saga.* Athens, Georgia: University of Georgia Press, 1984.

Lucas, S. Emmett, Jr. *Records of Effingham County, Georgia.* Easley, S.C.: Southern Historical Press, 1976.

Magazines

Griffin, Willie Llew. "A Forgotten Patriot." *Daughters of the American Revolution Magazine.* Vol. 98, No. 9 November 1964: 892-893.

Suddeth, Ruth Elgin. "Patriot in Oblivion." *Georgia Magazine*. Volume 1, No. 3, October-November 1957: 16-18.

CLIPPINGS

Anderson, Martha B. "New Bridge Links S.C.-Georgia." *The Hampton County Guardian* 21 Sept 1960:7.

Clark, Judge Richard H. (from "Memoirs") "Mysteries of Georgia's First Governor." *The Atlanta Journal* 21 June 1931:8A. Introduction to article states the late judge wrote his memoirs many years ago.

Daniel, Frank. "Georgia's Heroes to Be Unveiled." *The Atlanta Journal* 6 Mar 1960:1C and 6C.

Mallory, Rebah. "Monument to Georgia's First Governor - Effingham's John Adam Treutlen - Unveiled at Salzburger Meeting, Labor Day." *The Springfield Herald*. 6 Sept 1963:1.

Quick, Ruby Royal. "Who Killed Governor Treutlen? Mystery Unsolved." *The Augusta Chronicle* 1 Feb 1962:9C.

Rutherford, Marjory. "Duel Ends Famed Feud." *The Atlanta Constitution* 23 May 1961:10.

"10 Greatest Events in Georgia History." *The Atlanta Journal* 26 Apr 1936:8-9.

PHOTOSTATIC COPIES OF ARTICLES

Backtracking in Barbour County, Alabama: 155. Copy of this page from a book with no author or publisher identified was sent to Rebah Mallory in a letter by John B. Pridgen, Jr., a Treutlen descendant.

Caldwell, A.B. "John Adam Treutlen." *Men of Mark in Georgia*, edited by William J. Northen. A.B. Caldwell, Atlanta:1907:319-322.

Cook, James F. Ph.D. "First of a Series: Governors of Georgia Bulloch, Gwinnett and Treutlen." *Georgia Journal* Spring 1988:14-16.

Harrell, Bob. "Mystery Man." This is a copy of a newspaper or magazine article titled "Georgia History by Bob Harrell."

There are four articles attached to one page. "Dedication Program Set for Nov. 2." *West Chatham/Effingham Close Up* 24 Oct 1991. "HES Plans Dedication." *The Herald* 9 Oct 1991. "HES Meeting." *The Herald* 16 Oct 1991. "HES Honors Gov. Treutlen." *The Herald* 6 Nov 1991. All of these articles concern the dedication of Governor John Adam Treutlen Highway.

PRINTED PROGRAMS

Dedication Ceremony of "Governor John Adam Treutlen Highway" Central Junior High School Gym. 20 Mar 1978. It contains a portion of the Georgia resolution naming the highway.

"The Hall of Fame for Illustrious Georgians" at State Capitol, Atlanta, Georgia. 19 Mar 1960. This program booklet includes a picture of the Treutlen marble bust unveiled at that time and the inscription that accompanies it.

Program Meeting of Historical Effingham Society 2 Nov 1991 at Springfield United Methodist Church. The Governor John Adam Treutlen Highway at Tuckasee King. This program concluded with "Unveiling Highway Markers."

LETTERS

Douglass, Mary D. Note to Julia (Exley) Rahn. 20 Nov 1995. This memo is about monument to Treutlen in S.C.

Foy, J. Treutlen. Letter to Rebah Mallory. 6 Sept 1963. This letter concerns idea of naming bridge and placing marker.

Gnann, Otto. Letter to Julia (Exley) Rahn. 27 July 1995. This letter is about visit to possible gravesite of Treutlen.

Goff, John H. Letter to Rebah Mallory 26 Aug 1965. This letter contains sketch of a plat, resurveyed for John Adam Treutlen, 10 July 1769.

Helmly, I. Clinton, Jr. Letter to Rebah Mallory. 27 Feb 1961. This letter concerns proposed historical marker for the Georgia side of the bridge that crosses the Savannah River near Clyo.

Mallory, R.B. Letter to Milda Koppe. 4 Nov 1933. This letter is about a tree to be uprooted from Treutlen land and planted in Atlanta in honor of Treutlen.

Mallory, Rebah. Letter to (Mrs. W.G.) Pearl Gnann from Rebah asking where three pieces of information could be found. Pearl wrote the sources by the questions and mailed the letter back 14 Apr 1961. The information came from a book by W.J. Finck. Pearl promised to send the book to Rebah by a friend.

Soper, Michael. Letter to Rebah Mallory. 13 May 1961. This letter concerns naming the bridge and placing marker.

Treutlen, John Adam. Letter to John Hancock, June 19, 1777, telling him that Treutlen was sending General McIntosh under guard to Philadelphia. Photostatic copy is in Georgia Historical Society Library. Original is in Library of Congress.

Waldhouer, Jacob C. Letter to Senior Henry Muhlenberg, March 18, 1783, about Treutlen's third marriage and his death. Letter is in *Georgia Historical Quarterly* Vol. 49.

Zoe. Letter to Rebah Mallory. 26 Oct 1933. This letter was probably from Rebah's cousin Zoe Coburn. It concerns the tree to be planted to honor Treutlen.

Hand Written or Typed Material

Graham, Betty M. Undated one page article about death of Treutlen, as told to her by her grandmother, Kate, who heard it from her grandfather, Moses Metzger, a son of David Metzger.

Lewis, Bessie and Rebah Mallory. "John Adam Treutlen." Proposed text for Treutlen marker.
Mallory, Rebah. [Bridge]. 27 July 1961. This article had no heading. It was written for the *Savannah Morning News* with proposal to name the bridge in honor of Treutlen.

Mallory, Rebah Elizabeth. "Ancestor's Services." This is a copy of information sent to national DAR headquarters for membership in DAR.

Mallory, Rebah. "Governor John Adam Treutlen." 7 Aug 1975. This is a typed copy of information about Treutlen listing Gladys M. Layfield and Rebah E. Mallory as descendants. The exact information is found in a photostatic copy of an article, with author omitted, published in the *Sylvannia Telephone* 7 Aug 1975, headlined "Men of the Revolution Governor John Adam Treutlen," credited: "Contributed by the Brier Creek Chapter DAR." Gladys and Rebah were members of this chapter.

Mallory, Rebah and Edna Morgan. "John Adam Treutlen." Rebah's handwritten copy of article in *History of Effingham County, Georgia, 1731-1976*, published by Bicentennial Committee.

Mallory, Rebah. "Old Brick Ploughed up From Site of Red Brick Mansion of Georgia's First Governor John Adam Treutlen, on Savannah River, near Sister's Ferry at Clyo." 18 June 1938. Notation on back of last page Brick Atlanta Magazine Section — written on a slant one word under the other.

Mallory, Rebah. Sketch of John Adam Treutlen (One of Effingham County, Georgia's Heroes) (A Staunch Salzburger) (A Revolutionary Patriot)

Unidentified author or publisher. "John Adam Treutlen - Georgia's First Governor." These five pages of typed material, complete with bibliography and numbers in text referring to sources, must have been copied by Rebah or someone else because this is not Rebah's style of writing.

DEEDS, MAPS, AND PLATS

Deed to Treutlen's grant in South Carolina, formerly owned by R. B. Mallory, Sr. New private owner. Shown on page 8.

Maps of Savannah River. South Carolina Department of Archives and History. Columbia, S.C. Shown on pages 24 and 25.

Plat of Treutlen's South Carolina grant. Ibid. Shown on Page 9.

Plat of 93 acres showing house, 1769. Georgia Department of Archives and History. Atlanta, GA. Shown on page 7.

Plat of William Kennedy's estate. Effingham County Court House. Plat book C pages 227 and 228. Shown on pages 12 and 13.

Index

Index List
Name, Page(s)